Justus Jonas, Michael Caelius

Two Funeral Sermons on the Death of Dr. Martin Luther

Delivered at Eisleben, February 19th and 20th, 1546

Justus Jonas, Michael Caelius

Two Funeral Sermons on the Death of Dr. Martin Luther
Delivered at Eisleben, February 19th and 20th, 1546

ISBN/EAN: 9783337412784

Printed in Europe, USA, Canada, Australia, Japan

Cover: Foto ©Lupo / pixelio.de

More available books at **www.hansebooks.com**

TWO

FUNERAL SERMONS

ON THE DEATH OF

DR. MARTIN LUTHER,

Delivered at Eisleben, February 19th and 20th, 1546,

—BY—

DR. JUSTUS JONAS,

—AND—

PASTOR MICHAEL CELIUS.

TRANSLATED BY

REV. E. GREENWALD, D. D.,

PASTOR EVAN. LUTHERAN CHURCH OF THE HOLY TRINITY, LANCASTER, PA.

LANCASTER, PA.
PUBLISHED BY THE JUNIOR MISSIONARY SOCIETY
OF THE CHURCH OF THE HOLY TRINITY.
1883.

THE NEW ERA BOOK PRINT,
No. 3 South Queen Street,
LANCASTER, PA.

PREFACE.

A GENTLEMAN, a resident of Lancaster, of fine antiquarian tastes, who has accumulated a large library of valuable books, dating far back in the history of the art of printing, kindly presented to the Library of the Evan. Lutheran Church of the Holy Trinity, for the use of its pastors forever, among other books, a small volume containing the two funeral sermons preached by DR. JONAS and PASTOR CELIUS, at Eisleben, before the body of Luther was removed to Wittenberg for burial. The young people of the Junior Missionary Society of the Church, being made aware of the fact, and desirous of properly commemorating the four hundreth anniversary of Luther, conceived the idea of publishing an English translation of these sermons. In accordance with their wishes the translation was undertaken, and the book is herewith presented to the Church, as a suitable contribution to the literature appropriate to this year of its history.

DR. JONAS was a Professor at Wittenberg, an intimate friend of Luther, and accompanied him to the Diet of Worms, was at the Conference at Marburg, and at the Diet of Augsburg. He also went with Luther to Eisleben, and was present at his death. He assisted Luther in the translation of the Bible, and was eminent for his learning.

M. MICHAEL CELIUS was pastor of the church at Mansfeld, was very attentive to his beloved guest, and waited on him in his last hours. His sermon is a noble tribute to a great man.

Some of the expressions in these sermons may sound harsh to our ears, but these men were in earnest, and did not hesitate in the use of terms to express their true sentiments. We must also consider that they espoused the reformation at the hazard of their lives. Imprisonment and death stared them in the face, and they risked their all for their principles. Romanism was savage and blood-thirsty, and Luther, and the adherents of the Reformation, would have been cruelly murdered, if their protectors, the Electors of Saxony, had not defended them from the malice of the papists. It is, perhaps, difficult for us to fully conceive the intense bitterness of the hate with which Luther and the Reformation were pursued by their enemies. These sermons describe their character in terms not stronger than their character warranted.

These sermons, preached in the presence of the corpse of Luther, and before large congregations of his deeply affected friends, furnish very interesting and instructive reading.

E. G.

LANCASTER, PA., April 16, 1883.

THE FIRST SERMON,

By Dr. Justus Jonas, on the death of Dr. Martin Luther, delivered at Eisleben, February 19, 1546, and repeated afterwards at Halle.*

I. Thess. 4: 13-18. But I would not have you to be ignorant, brethren, concerning them which are asleep, that ye sorrow not, even as others which have no hope. For if we believe that Jesus died and rose again, even so them also which sleep in Jesus will God bring with him. For this we say unto you by the word of the Lord, that we which are alive and remain unto the coming of the Lord, shall not prevent them which are asleep. For the Lord himself shall descend from heaven with a shout, with the voice of the archangel, and with the trump of God: and the dead in Christ shall rise first: then we which are alive and remain shall be caught up with them in the clouds, to meet the Lord in the air: and so shall we ever be with the Lord. Wherefore comfort one another with these words.

Dearly Beloved:

We have Christian reasons for delivering this sermon on the death of our dear father Dr. Martin Luther, who with so great fidelity and zeal labored for the comfort and welfare of the whole of Christendom, and particularly of all the churches of the entire German nation. You, here at Halle, were especially beloved by him, and your welfare lay near his heart. Through him a large part of the world has been converted from error to truth. Seven weeks ago, to-day, the dear man of God peacefully fell asleep in Christ, at Eisleben, his native place, shortly before three o'clock in the morning. The

*Taken down in short hand at the time of delivery.

next day I preached a sermon in St. Andrew's church at Eisleben, with tears that could not be restrained, the corpse having been placed in the centre of the church before me. It was preached, as is the present discourse, in order to remind devout Christian souls what a treasure they possessed for a time, in the life, and have now lost, in the death, of this dear eminent man. I then divided the sermon into three parts, namely:

FIRST: *Of the person of Dr. Martin Luther,* his great gifts, and his profound understanding of spiritual things. Particularly how he had, for more than a year past, made preparation for his peaceful death.

SECOND: *Of the resurrection of the dead,* and that we will certainly again see and hear, at the Judgment Day, in eternal joy and felicity, the man, Dr. Martin Luther, who for more than twenty-nine years wrote and contended for us against the Kingdom of the devil, the diabolical falsehoods of the pope, and the corruptions of the monks.

THIRD: Of the assurance that *the death of Dr. Martin Luther,* like that of all the holy prophets, *will have special power, and be followed by blessed effects,* in the conflict with the godless, hardened, and benighted papists.

First, the knowledge of the person and splendid gifts of Dr. Martin Luther, of blessed memory, and how gently and well he prepared himself for death, affords great consolation to all God-fearing men. I heartily wish, because it is worth wishing, that you all who are present, here in this church, had just come from the fresh perusal of the Book of Genesis, as so ably and well expounded by our dear father, Dr. Martin Luther, and also that you had just read, as many no doubt have, and retained freshly in remembrance, his exposition of the 14th, 15th, 16th and 17th chapters of St. John's Gospel. Only then would you rightly comprehend what a great man, and rich treasure, you have lost in the death of Dr. Martin Luther. No Doctors of Paris, Lyons, or other distinguished Universities, are capable of preparing an exposition equal to Luther's German explanation of the Epistle to the Galatians, the Psalms, the Proverbs of Solomon, or the Book of Ecclesiastes. Indeed, all the papists melted together could not do it. These, and other books of his, show how great a man Dr. Luther was, how richly he was endowed, and how diligently and faithfully he labored with the Word of God. From this, too, we learn how great a man we have lost.

Of Luther, as an individual, we have much to say, but it is impossible for me to say all that might be said. We will therefore pass over the acute genius, and the admirable, quick understanding, which our dear father, Dr. Martin Luther, of blessed, Christian memory, possessed even from his youth; in the 18th and 20th year of his age. I have heard many persons, who have had much intercourse with him from his youth, testify that they never knew a more highly gifted person. Among

them are Dr. Lang and Dr. Staupitz of Erford. They
knew him well, as they had daily intercourse with him
for a long time. The same may be said of Dr. Weller-
stadt, who was Rector of the University of Wittenberg
when it was founded, and who testified of Luther as
follows: "Take care of the young monk, M. Martin
Luther; he has an excellent acute mind, the like of
which I have never before in my life met with; he will
certainly become an eminent man." So, too, it has come
to pass.

Dr. Martin Luther also possessed many other eminent
gifts. He was an extremely powerful orator. Particularly, he was a most able interpreter of the entire Bible.
Even the officials of the court have, in part, learned
from him to speak and write pure German. For he has
restored the German language, so that the people again
read and write the German language correctly, as many
in the higher ranks of society are compelled to acknowledge and testify. How eloquent a man, and eminent a
writer, Dr. Martin Luther was, we often learn from little
things, as from his letters. However, his numerous
books and other writings sufficiently prove it. The
master is known by his work. Of his extraordinary
natural talents I will say nothing, only I will refer all
God-fearing and devout Christians to his books, postils,
and commentaries for proof. They will learn from
them what an eminent orator, preacher, and bishop
they have had in him. Would to God Germany had

many such men and bishops, for she needs them much.

Dr. Martin Luther also possessed, in large measure, the grace of God, the illumination of the Holy Ghost, and the true knowledge of God and Christ. These gracious gifts were not permitted to decline in him, but he increased them daily, by the diligent use of the holy divine Scriptures, their careful study, and the devout reading of them for forty years. He was well acquainted with the entire Bible, which he read through so many times that the whole was clear to his mind. This habit the good, dear man, pursued steadily from his 24th until his 63d year, and until he died.

I must here recall two expressions of his which reveal his inmost heart. Our Lord says: "Out of the abundance of the heart the mouth speaketh." The first expression is this: "I heartily wish that I understood something of the first Article of the Christian Creed which says: 'I believe in God the Father, Almighty Maker of heaven and earth.' But I will willingly remain an A B C learner in this article, and I hold that few people, even the eminent, except Adam, Noah, Abraham, David, have understood it. But Isaiah, Jeremiah, and other Patriarchs and Prophets have understood something of it, but all these have studied thereat until they have acknowledged themselves to be as yet only learners."

The other expression is this: "I would that the second Article, which treats of Redemption, (that God sent

His Son into the world to redeem the whole human race,) was regarded as the highest Theology, the same as St. Paul and all the Apostles regarded it." He saw and understood well what a sublime and excellent article of faith that is, which declares that God sent His Son into the world to redeem it, and that so long as a man lives he will have enough to do, to study and learn about it, and yet not exhaust the subject. Many such famous Theological schools as Paris, Cologne, and others, have, however, given the least attention to it, and have even taught idle human opinions in opposition to it. Of this more hereafter.

We will now speak about the manner in which Dr. Martin Luther, a whole year before his end, made preparation so as to be ready for death. As he attained his sixty-third year, he spoke often such precious words as may well be compared to the preaching of Noah. He also lived in very evil times, and said with pain at heart, "Oh, the world loves lies, as those of the pope, the monks, and other human fables, and is so set against the clear light of the Gospel, that by many persons, not mere common sins are practiced, but such great wickedness as blasphemy against God, misuse of God's name, scoffing at sacred things, and the known persistence in gross vices. No one, any longer, is willing to be a poor sinner, and none will humble himself before God. Chastisement is sure to follow."

It is an evidence of special grace and knowledge of

God on the part of Luther, that he made ready for his departure an entire year before it took place. He wrote in his Psalter and Pocket Prayer Book, which he always carried with him, more than twenty consolatory passages, as much as to say: "I will, with the help of God, lay hold of one of these passages in my last hour, and be armed against the assaults of the devil, and all the gates of hell." And the passages written in his Pocket Prayer Book show that he was not a novice, but a master in spiritual conflicts.

The first passage which he wrote down for his spiritual comfort, is i. Peter 5 : 7, "Casting all your care upon him, for he careth for you." As if he would say: Gather together all your cares and anxieties into one bundle; inclose the very greatest of your cares in one grasp, (as the Greek word epirritsantes carries with it the meaning,) and cast them upon him, transfer them to Christ, who cares for you.

Applying this precious and consoling passage to his own case, the dear, devout man, Dr. Martin, cast all his cares upon the Lord Jesus Christ, in the hour of death, and neither asked nor felt concern, as to where he would be. On the contrary, he let God care for his soul, which he committed into his hands, confident that he would take care of it and save it. All men are anxious, when they die, as to what will become of them. But here we learn that God will take care of us during all our lives, and especially in our highest need, namely,

in the hour of death, and in the last extremity. It is
true, I could not have applied this passage of St. Peter,
so consolingly, to the last dying hour, but we see here
what an extraordinary man, Dr. Martin was, and how
diligently he had searched the apostle's words.

On this passage, our dear father penned these
thoughts: Our dear faithful God, who has put me into
the high office of the ministry, will surely care for me,
and keep my soul safely. I will, therefore, with confi-
dence and joy, commend my spirit into His hands. For
the Lord will know well where my soul shall abide, since
He has so loved it, and cared for it, that He gave His
life, yea his own soul, in order to redeem my soul. He
is the noblest and best Shepherd and Bishop of all the
souls that believe in Him; blessed be he forever! He
has not need to begin in me, to learn how He shall care
for believing Christian souls. I know I will not be the
first, on whom God will learn how he shall protect and
keep the souls that believe in Christ. Saint Lorentz
commended his soul to Christ on the glowing gridiron,
and said: "Christ has cared for my soul; He will keep
it safely." In the same way St. Stephen committed his
soul to Christ, as he was being stoned to death, and said:
"Lord Jesus, receive my spirit," Acts 7:59, and by Him
his soul was taken up, and received to eternal life. And
many martyrs more, so that I am not the first who commended himself to Christ, and whose soul was safely
kept. I would not be willing, (he often said,) that the

salvation of my soul should be in my own hands. For
if it depended on me, my soul would long ago, and in a
moment, have been torn to destruction by Satan, as a
young chicken, or a little bird, by the talons of a hawk.
But neither devil nor man can wrest my soul out of the
hands of Christ, to whose keeping I have committed it.
Christ says, John 10:27–29, "My sheep hear my voice,
and they follow me, and no man is able to pluck them
out of my, or my Father's, hand."

So, too, our dear father wrote in his Psalter the sentence of St. Ambrose, in which he said to his brethren:
"I trust that I have not lived among you so that I would
dread to live among you longer, for we have a good and
faithful Lord, and I know no friend who has cared for
me more constantly than He. Therefore, also, I am not
afraid to die." By this sentence from St. Ambrose our
dear Dr. Luther would indicate that he too did not
dread to live longer in the world, for he had lived so he
had no cause to be ashamed of his life and conversa-
tion; and that, at the same time, he had no fears of
death, when it should be God's will to call him hence,
for he knew that he had in heaven a mansion of rest,
which Christ had acquired and appointed for him.

Further, he wrote in his Psalter the words of a very
godly bishop, who might well be compared to St. Ambrose, to whom the wickedness of the world caused
much pain, and which he could scarcely endure. To
him gave Jesus the answer in his last hours, and said:

"Thou weepest and mournest; has the world dealt so well with thee that thou art reluctant to leave it? Thou canst not endure the wickedness of the world, and yet thou art not willing to part from it." This sentence Dr. Luther did not write without reason. O how much sorrow and suffering did his enemies cause him, and how it distressed his heart, that the world continued to be so godless, sunk in avarice, love of usury, contempt of God's Word, and unthankfulness for it, in envy, hatred, and the Satanic venom of popery. Particularly it distressed him, that so many brethren were false, and fell away from the true doctrine; and on this account, he would willingly die, and lie down in the grave.

He also loved the sentence: Why fearest thou to be with Jesus, who has evinced for thee the greatest faithfulness, in that He made His soul an offering for thy redemption, and died for thee on the cross? Thinkest thou that the Devil, or the world, would have done for thee, what Christ has done? Wherewith does the world show such faithfulness? This the world does not. Why therefore, dost thou desire to remain here? The world has not given body and soul for thee, but Jesus Christ, the Son of God, has sacrificed himself for thy salvation. Thou canst, therefore, reach, and abide at, no place where it will be better with thee, than with the Lord Jesus Christ, the Son of God, who has suffered and died for thee. No more exquisitively beautiful sentiment, or one more worthy of record, could he have marked for himself.

The following passage also stands written in his Pocket Prayer Book: "Matthew 19:17, 'If thou wilt enter into life, keep the commandments,' i. e. die. For it is appointed unto all men once to die. Therefore, if thou wilt act according to this passage, and enter into life, die, and thou hast kept God's commandment, and wilt live. For the present life is a life of sin, and of the penalty laid upon sin, and we do not cease to sin until we die. He, therefore, that has died happily, and in Christ, is free from sin, and need no longer fear the punishment of sin. On the contrary, he is released and free from all the misery, tribulation, and distresses of this mortal life." In this way he ingeniously explained and applied the passage. Who would have thought to expound, in so masterly a way, this expression, Keep God's commandments, as that it means, to die?

From these, and many other consolatory passages which he wrote down, we learn how very thoughtful and devout a man our dear father Dr. Martin was, in that, for more than an entire year before his death, he made special preparation for it, as if he would say: I must hence; I will keep God's commandments; I must depart this life and leave this evil world; I will therefore be ready to enter another life, and a world better than this. In the same spirit he said on Wednesday evening, a few hours only before he peacefully fell asleep, "When I shall have reconciled my dear countrymen, the Counts Mansfeld, here in Eisleben, I will return home, and lay my body in the grave, to be food for the worms." These words indicate that he had thought much of death, and the hour of his own dying, and that he did not dread his departure from this life. All these passages enable us well to understand what a precious, exalted spirit he was of, and so dear, and full of the spirit of God, that the world for ages had not his equal.

This will suffice, in brief, for the first part of my discourse on the person of Dr. Martin. I will now proceed to the second part.

The second part of this sermon will be On the Resurrection of the Dead, when at the last day we shall again see our dear father, and reverend Dr. Martin Luther, who has been taken from us by death. St. Paul says plainly in the text, that "those that sleep in Jesus will God bring with him." The Christian comforts himself with these words, and he that is not comforted by them may not presume to think himself a Christian. This text is so rich and consoling as to be more precious than gold. A Christian holds fast to this truth, derives great comfort from it, and believes firmly that he, with all other Christians, will rise again at the last day. An ungodly, Epicurean swine finds no comfort in the words of St. Paul. He finds pleasure only in his gold and possessions, his avarice and usury. For he neither knows nor believes that he will rise again at the last day, or that he will again see those who now live with him, or who have lived before him. St. Paul, however, says: "The Lord himself shall descend from heaven with a shout, with the voice of the archangel, and with the trump of God." The Lord is great, and great, too, must be His triumph and glory. But an Epicurean does not concern himself with these words, and does not take them to himself. To a true Christian heart, however, they are pure pearls, and most precious treasures. St. Paul held this doctrine to be a great and special mystery, of which the world knew nothing, which he here uttered to Christians concerning the resurrection of the dead. And he concludes his statement with the words: "Comfort one another with these words." As if he would say, Behold, I will reveal to you a heavenly mystery, namely, the world, and all men whom ye see in it, old and young, rich and poor, must descend to the dust. That is, they must die and be buried, as well the Christian as he that is not a Christian. But after this, at the last day, flesh and blood, notwithstanding they had been eaten of worms, and had rotted and decayed in the ground, shall again come forth and rise in great glory, as St. Paul in the 15th chapter of First Corinthians has clearly made known to us: "It is sown in corruption, it is raised in incorruption: it is sown in dishonor, it is raised in glory."

When, therefore, a dear friend dies, we may have the consolation to see him again at the last day. In the same way, St. Paul comforted himself in view of the imprisonment and death that awaited him from the cruel and

blood-thirsty tyrant, Nero, at Rome. Even though he
should be tortured and put to death, he, with all men,
would rise again at the last day. So, too, all the children that are born, or that are yet to be born, (for this
life consists of being born, living and dying,) will, with
their bodies, rise again. A joyful, happy day will come,
the day of redemption, as Jesus calls it in Luke 21:28.
After the vicissitudes of life and death a joyful day will
come. There will then be no more marrying or giving
in marriage, no more birth of children, no more becom-
ing lame, blind or sick, no more death, for mortality
shall cease, and an immortal, everlasting life shall begin
to be.

St. Paul further says: "And the dead in Christ shall
rise first. Then we which are alive and remain, shall be
caught up together with them in the clouds to meet the
Lord in the air: and so shall we ever be with the Lord."

This is a beautiful, golden text, and great comfort is in
it for Christians, which we may cherish all our life long,
and with which we may console ourselves amid all
earth's sorrows. The Lord shall descend from heaven
with a shout, says St. Paul, we shall arise from the
dead, and ever be with the Lord. Of this the world
knows nothing, neither rejoices in it, nor comforts itself
with it, but finds its pleasure only in its money and goods.
St. Paul intends by these words to say: My dear Christians, although you should lose me, who am your bishop,
minister and shepherd in Christ, who cares for your

souls, nevertheless, I will rise again, and will certainly
see you again as my spiritual children in yonder world,
and you will see me, likewise, forever.

He says: Christ will come with a shout. This shout
will be loud, and will be made by the voice of the archangel, and the trump of God. It will awake the dead.
Then they that have gone to sleep in Jesus, in the true,
pure faith, will rise first. Afterwards, they that are alive
will be caught up together with them in the clouds. So also
Jesus says, John 5:28–29: "Verily, verily I say unto you,
the hour is coming, when all that are in their graves
shall hear his voice, and shall come forth, they that have
done good unto the resurrection of life, and they that have
done evil to the resurrection of damnation." Together
with the first will our dear father, Dr. Martin Luther,
of blessed memory, also rise with the same body, face,
hands, feet, which he had and as we saw him here, and
with the blessed lips, which for twenty-nine whole years
preached God's word purely to the people of Germany.
But he will come forth with a glorified body, that will
shine as the sun, as Christ has said, Matthew 13:43:
"Then shall the righteous shine forth as the sun in the
Kingdom of their Father;" and, as Daniel has foretold,
12:3: "They that be wise shall shine as the brightness
of the firmament, and they that have turned many to
righteousness as the stars for ever and ever." As now Dr.
Martin was a wise and great teacher who turned many,
very many to righteousness, he will also shine as the stars
before others, and, so God will, we too will see him.

Job says, Chap. 19:25-26: "I know that my Redeem-
er liveth, and that he shall stand at the latter day upon
the earth, and though after my skin worms destroy this
body, yet in my flesh shall I see God." It is a great
comfort for Christians to know that they will rise with
their bodies from the dead, and in their flesh shall see
God. In this passage, Job says in all respects the same
things that St. Paul says concerning the resurrection.
In this resurrection, at the last day, we will see the great
and dear man whom we have now lost, Dr. Luther, and
not see him alone, but he will also again kindly converse
with us, whom he knew on earth, to whom he preached,
whom through God's Word he converted, and not with
us alone, but also with the whole heavenly host, with
the holy Patriarchs and Prophets, concerning the severe conflict and strife which he maintained with the Kingdom of Satan, and from which he suffered so much in the
world, during the twenty-nine years of violent assaults
arrayed against him. Dr. Martin Luther had many
fierce contests with the Devil, particularly in the great
affair of Carlstadt, in the weighty matters debated in the
Diet of Augsburg, in the great concerns of the Sacra-
ments, of the Anabaptists, of the Antinomians, and
others. Dr. Martin himself often said: "What I had to
bear and suffer on account of the doctrine of the dear
Gospel of Christ, which God has now revealed anew to
the world, there shall no human being learn from me
here in this world, but at the great day it will be made

known." At the last day, then, will he tell us, and we will learn what he would not here reveal to any one, of the great victories of the Son of God against sin, the Devil, the papists and false brethren, accomplished by him. All this will he then tell us, as we shall be together, and make known to us the glorious revelations he received when he began to preach the Gospel, as will fill us with wonder, and lead us to praise God for the victories which he gained, as is said in Psalm 84:7: "They go from strength to strength." (German, "They gain one victory after another.") But of this no Satanic monk or stiff-necked papist knows one word. And even if they read it in the Scriptures, they nevertheless believe it not.

The resurrection of the dead, will quickly come. They who are asleep in Christ first, and then they who are alive shall be caught up together with them in the clouds, to meet the Lord in the air, and so shall they ever be with the Lord. Would to God such day of the Lord would come soon, and that it would happen that we would be caught up to meet the Lord before we sat down to table, and be released from the suffering and distress which we must endure here in this evil world, and an end be made to the faithlessness of the world, the insatiable usury, avarice, envy, slander, pomp, pride, and other vices, together with the dreadful blasphemy and contempt of sacred things, the persecutions, murder and blood-shedding, the idolatry of the desperate, ungodly papists, monks and nuns. These things they practice everywhere, and in the grossest forms.

For the coming of such a blessed day, we should continually pray. Ah, the last day would be a blessed, joyful day, since then each would know the other better than in this wretched life, the wife her husband, the husband the wife, the children their parents, the minister his hearers, and would without ceasing speak with each other, be together, adore and praise God together, in the great general assembly and Church in heaven, with the holy angels, for ever and ever.

This, says St. Paul to the Thessalonians, ye will scarcely believe, or only with a feeble faith, for it is a sublime Article of the Christian Creed, that the putrefied bodies, or the bodies consumed by fire, shall rise again, know each other, speak with each other, and forever praise God. At this Article reason stumbles and takes offense, for it cannot understand how the body that the worms devour, or that is reduced by fire to powder and ashes, can again come forth, a living being. When the Article of the Resurrection of the dead is preached, the world laughs at it, and holds it to be the babbling of fools, as we see in Acts 17:18. When St. Paul at Athens preached the doctrine of the Resurrection of the dead, some began to mock, and say: "What will this babbler say?" So, too, when St. Paul spake before King Agrippa of the Resurrection of the dead, Festus exclaimed with a loud voice, "Paul, thou art beside thyself, much learning doth make thee mad." Acts 26:24.

We see from this how lightly the world esteems this Article, and calls those who preach it, babblers, beside themselves, and mad people, just as the Pope of Rome, the Bishops and Cardinals call us Germans fools and silly people, because we preach, believe, and surely hold, that we, with our dear ones, will rise again at the last day, and see God.

The mystery of the resurrection of the dead, our dear Lord has revealed by His holy Word and Gospel, which mystery the world ridicules; but the true Church and our suffering Christianity have in it its eternal living consolation. A Christian should recall every morning, when he arises from slumber, this precious, revealed mystery, and say to himself: "I know that a day will come, in which God will awaken all who are asleep in Christ, and that all our bodies will arise, those that have believed in Christ, and have done good, to eternal life. Thus should a Christian always keep in mind, and meditate upon that blessed day, and the coming again of Christ. It will make him more patient amid the various sufferings, crosses and persecutions he meets with in life.

The hardened, blind and wretched papists have not one single thought of this. Indeed, they slander and persecute the Holy Gospel, which reveals and makes known to us the great mystery of the Resurrection of the dead, which is material to the salvation of our souls, for whoever does not believe the doctrine concerning the Resurrection of the dead, hears the preaching of the Gospel in vain, believes in vain, remains in his sins, and will perish, as St. Paul teaches in I. Corinthians 15: 14–18. With such people, who slander the Gospel, who will not accept it, nor hear it, nor believe it, we should have nothing to do, but flee from and avoid them, as the Devil himself. For a hardened, obdurate papist has the very spirit of the devil. They have no faith; what they do believe comes in at the window and goes out at the door.

With these words St. Paul wishes to say to the Thessalonians: I have taught you the mystery of the Resurrection of the dead, as it will take place at the last day. But I, Paul, who have faithfully made known to you these things from God's Word and by His spirit, will not remain always here, and continue to be your minister. Nero will know how to prevent it. He will kill me, and I must cease to preach. Well, even if the world with great wrath shall put me to death, nevertheless at the last day I will rise again with you all, and you with me. With this assurance, the Thessalonians, with St. Paul, comforted themselves and rejoiced. This, too, comforted and gladdened the heart of our dear father, Dr. Martin Luther, the Prophet and Preacher of Germany. The thought was as precious to him, as it was to St. Paul, that although he would die and be buried, and be taken from us, his beloved hearers and spiritual children, into another and better life, nevertheless he would rise again at the last day, and see us forever in heavenly joy.

That we shall again see and hear our dear father and minister in a future, everlasting life, should also give us comfort and awaken joy. Thereto may God help us, through Jesus Christ. Amen. This may suffice, for this time, for the second part.

Third. We are to consider in this sermon: That the death of the great prophet, Dr. Martin, will certainly be followed by great results. For before two years are past we will find out, and, before others, will the papists, canons, priests, monks and nuns find out, although they rejoice on account of the death and removal of Dr. Martin Luther, that he will have left a great power behind him. In a few years they will wish that Dr. Luther yet lived, for then they would willingly obey him, and if they could, they would dig his body out of the earth. But they have delayed too long. Well would it have been for them, in body and soul, if in his lifetime they had heeded his warnings and followed his counsels.

We read in the Book of Chronicles that, always, when the times were evil, fast, perilous, and at the worst, then the greatest and most eminent prophets and men of God lived. For example, before the Deluge, Noah; before the burning and destruction of Sodom and Gomorrah, Lot; afterwards, Elijah, Elisha, &c. But always a great and fearful calamity followed soon after the death of each eminent prophet and holy man of God. So, too, we read in the Book of Judges. When Gideon died the Jews became godless, as recorded in the eighth chapter, v. 33: "The children of Israel turned again, and went a whoring after Baalim, and made Baal-berith their God." They set up idolatrous altars for the worship of Baal. Then quickly followed God's rod and chastisement. So, too, will God's terrible punishment assuredly fall upon Germany, after the death of the man of God, Dr. Martin, if it does not amend its ways. And particularly will His chastisements fall, without doubt, and before others, upon the godless, hardened, desperate papists, monks, priests and nuns.

The Biography of St. Augustine shows that he lived seventy years, nearly ten years longer than Dr. Martin Luther, and that he was forty years in the ministry, having preached ten years longer than Dr. Luther. As he was near his end, and about to die, he foresaw that Africa, his fatherland, would suffer great misfortune, and that things would go ill with the Church. He was greatly distressed thereat, as we are that evil should befall our German Country, after having enjoyed such clear light of the Gospel. But notwithstanding Augustine so greatly feared that after his death his fatherland would lose the Gospel, God so ordered that, for yet two hundred years afterwards, the pure word of God was preached in Africa. This took place in answer to prayer. As we too are, at this time, so greatly concerned, lest we should lose the Word of God, let us also begin to live penitently, and earnestly pray that God would preserve His Word yet longer among us, after Dr. Martin Luther's death, as He did in the time of St. Augustine. May the all-merciful God grant this, through Jesus Christ our Lord. Amen.

Oh how often and earnestly did the dear father, Dr. Martin Luther, admonish Germany to repent, and warn them of God's judgments, if they refused; as in his Houspostil on the Gospel of the Destruction of Jerusalem: Luke 19. He did the same in his Exposition of the 110th Psalm, also in his Book addressed to the ecclesiastics at Augsburg; and likewise in his Address to his beloved German Countrymen. He warned them that unless they amended their ways, abandoned their idolatry, shunned idolatrous people, and particularly renounced the ways of the ungodly papistical monks and nuns, and others like them, God would visit them with His sore judgments, take His word entirely from them, and suffer them to fall back into their former frightful errors. So he preached here at Halle, and most earnestly and faithfully uttered his warning voice. These warnings of this dear man and prophet should be laid well to heart; idolatry should be renounced; the old leaven cleaned out; the papistic idol worship and sin no longer participated in, so that we may not again lose the Word of God, which has been restored to us. Before all should the papists take especial heed, as those to whom these threatenings will come home, unless they amend their ways.

John Huss predicted, before they burned him, that one hundred years after him a swan would appear, whom they would be compelled to have, and whom they could not roast. This swan was no other than our dear father, Dr. Martin Luther, who has preached and told the Truth, plainly and unvarnished, to pope, bishops, cardinals, priests, monks, and to all the world, being afraid of no one. Him they were unable to roast or to destroy, however often they wished it, and would heartily have done it, but they failed of their purpose. He peacefully went to sleep in God, in his loved native city, Eisleben. As John Huss predicted, before his death, so it came to pass. Dr. Martin Luther often said, when they spoke to him about the papists and the monks: Well, be content; ask, after my death, where the monks and papists are. They will all be scattered and perished as the chaff is blown away by the wind, because they will not permit themselves to be instructed from God's word, and will not turn from their errors, but remain hardened in their falsehoods, idolatries and ungodly ways. No castigation, instruction, admonition nor entreaty will avail with them, as David complains in the 36th Psalm, and says, v. 4: "He setteth himself in a way that is not good." So truly do the papists "set themselves" in their evil ways. Therefore, it will also happen to them as is recorded in the 37th Psalm, vs. 35, 36: "I have seen the wicked in great power, and spreading himself like a green bay tree, yet he passed away, and lo, he was not: yea, I sought him, but he could not be found." So the papists are defiant, blown up with pride, and threaten to devour us, and particularly are they now greatly elated since our dear Luther is dead. Better would it be for them if they would let themselves be advised, and would repent. Then would they be helped and prospered in body and soul. But if they will not, God's eternal judgment and wrath will come upon them, namely, the damnation and fire of hell. For, says our Lord Jesus Christ, in His Gospel: "Except ye repent, ye shall all likewise perish." When they think themselves most secure are they suddenly, like the ungodly, swept away.

Our dear father, Dr. Martin Luther, has himself prepared an Epitaph, as well as prophecy, concerning popery, which reads thus: *Pestis eram vivens, moriens ero mors tua, Papa.* [Living I was thy plague, dying I will be thy death, O! pope.]

The papists may well see to it that they repent of having for twenty-nine entire years past, slandered, reviled, persecuted, condemned as heresy and doctrine of devils, the Gospel of Christ, and on account of it chased away, murdered, drowned and hanged Christians who believed and practiced it. It will be well if they henceforth begin to believe and accept, and help to further the Gospel; otherwise, as Luther was to them in life a plague, and by his writing and preaching pressed them hard, and alarmed them greatly, so after his death he will surely be the death and final extinguishment of their entire mockery, idolatry, and other abominations.　God grant that they may follow God's Word, be converted and, with us, believe and accept it and be saved at last.　Amen.

THE SECOND SERMON,

PREACHED IN PRESENCE OF THE CORPSE OF DR. MARTIN LUTHER
AT EISLEBEN, ON THE 20TH DAY OF FEBRUARY, 1546,
BY M. MICHAEL CELIUS.

We are here assembled to-day, at the call of God, and
in accordance with a wholesome ancient usage of the
Holy Christian Church, in the presence of the corpse of
that reverend man, and learned doctor, Martin Luther,
who died in the Lord, and is blessed. We have
cause heartily to lament his departure from us, and to
seek consolation for our sorrow. We will take as the
preface to this sermon, the passage from Isaiah, ch. 57:
1, 2:

"The righteous perisheth, and no man layeth it to
heart, and merciful men are taken away, none considering that the righteous is taken away from the evil to
come. He shall enter into peace. They shall rest in
their beds, each one walking in his uprightness."

I have chosen these words as a fit introduction to my
sermon, not that I propose to present everything includ-
ed in the sense and meaning of the prophet in these
verses. He here, and in the context, describes the true
and false teachers in the Church, who they are, what is
their character, and what their end. He speaks of false

and unrighteous teachers; they are watchmen, it is true, because they sit in the regular offices in the Church, as do now the pope and his cardinals, bishops, monks and priests. But they are "blind watchmen." "They are all ignorant," "that cannot understand" the scriptures, nor the mysteries of the holy Gospel. In addition to this "they are all dumb dogs that cannot bark, sleeping, lying down, loving to slumber." At the same time, "they are greedy dogs which can never have enough; they all look to their own way, every one for his gain." They live in all manner of voluptuousness, and for a reward they will suffer the fires of hell.

But the genuine and true teachers, of whom our dear master and father in Christ, Dr. Martin Luther, was one, are the righteous; that is, they truly know God in His Word, teach and preach the righteousness of faith, together with good works, as He has commanded. These do not see many good days in the world, which does not rest until they are taken away and destroyed. But the prophet concludes, "they shall enter into peace, and they shall rest in their beds." But not dwelling on this now, we must accept the sad leave-taking of this corpse, and as St. Paul allowed the Thessalonians to sorrow, but not without Christian hope and consolation, I propose to confine my remarks to the consideration of what a great man and teacher Dr. Martin Luther was, how he died, why he fell asleep in the Lord just at this time, and what, until the day of the Lord, his state and condition will be.

When any are about to describe a man of the world, they usually inquire, Was he of an honorable family? Who were his ancestors? What were their standing? their dignities? their condition? What virtues and good qualities did he possess? How did he employ them? and what did he accomplish in life? To have, in these respects, a good reputation is a divinely great gift, and for its proper employment and right use we may well thank God.

Much, in all these respects, can be said of this dear man, Dr. Martin Luther. He, perhaps, derived his lineage, name and descent from the Emperor Luther. Or, it may be that, as in the case of so many families in the world, who rise and fall in respectability, just as David's race had fallen in the time of Christ, so that Isaiah compared it to an old, dry tree, the family of our dear master and father may also no longer be in high consideration. But this city of Eisleben, and the entire county of Mansfeld, know that he was descended from honorable and godly parents, that he was legitimately born here in Eisleben, that he was baptized as a Christian, that when he was six months old his parents removed with him to Mansfeld, where they passed the greater part of their lives, with honor. There both father and mother peacefully fell asleep in Christ, confessing their faith, and calling on the name of the Lord; the evidence of which this dear man of God put into my own hands. To God's grace be all the glory.

So we could say much in his praise, on account of his many noble virtues. That he loved and practiced the strictest temperance and good morals, no one can say aught in contradiction. But I will leave to others of greater ability to speak and write of these, and other virtues, and for this time I will confine myself to the spiritual office to which God called him, which he filled in the Church, and to the blessing which the+holy Christian Church enjoyed in him. It will admonish you to love him.

No one who knows and loves God's Word and truth, will doubt that this man, whose corpse we yet see here before us, filled the office in the Church, which, in their time, Elijah and Jeremiah, John the Baptist, or one of the Apostles, filled. For if these were endowed of God with peculiar divine gifts before him, yet, so far as belonged to the office, he was, in our time, truly a real Elijah or Jeremiah, and before the coming of the great day of the Lord, he was a John the Forerunner, or an Apostle.

Whosoever will acknowledge the truth, must admit that the Church was in the same state when God awakened and called this man, as it was in the time of the prophets Elijah and Jeremiah, and when God sent out John and the Apostles to preach. The Scriptures say, I. Kings, 18th chapter, that in the time of the prophet Elijah the entire nation of Israel had fallen from God, and had attached themselves to the idolatrous worship of Baal—

that Elijah lamented that he alone remained a prophet of the Lord in Israel, and that all the rest had fallen away, and served, the one this, and the other another, god. The true God had not more than one prophet; Baal had four hundred and fifty. And the prophets of the groves that ate at Jezebel's table numbered four hundred.

So, too, in the time of Jeremiah, God complained of His people, chapter 2, and said, "Ye have made my heritage an abomination. The priests said not, Where is the Lord? and they that handle the law knew me not; the pastors also transgressed against me, and the prophets prophesied by Baal, and walked after things that do not profit. Wherefore, I will yet plead with you, saith the Lord, and with your children's children will I plead."

In what condition the Church was in the time of John the Baptist, appears very clearly from the New Testament. Whilst, after the Babylonish captivity idol worship was not set up as before, yet the people were split up into sects, and there were Essenes, Pharisees and Sadducees, and each considered itself better than the others, each relied upon its own good works, and as the Prophet described them, "worshipped the work of their own hands." On this account, the Prophet Jeremiah lamented exceedingly, and cried out against them. Elijah, however, put to death in one day all the priests of Baal. John called them serpents and a "generation of vipers." They all attack, with a zealous spirit, all their idolatrous ways, overturn their idols, and establish again the true doctrine of repentance and forgiveness of sin, and teach the true way of serving God.

In the same sad state, my dear friends, has been the Holy Christian Church in the last days, under the papal Antichrist. There the dregs of all the abominable errors, heresies, sects, and idolatries had flowed together in one mass. There was no true knowledge of the Holy Scriptures; no true doctrine to comfort the conscience was preached; human dogmas were esteemed higher than God's Word; no one knew how to call upon God, of whom, in our need, we are to expect deliverance; what we should do or how we should serve Him. Darkness covered the whole earth; no light shone in the Church; in short, as the Prophet Ezekial says, chapter 34:5-6: "My sheep are scattered because there is no shepherd: they wandered through all the mountains, and none did search and ask after them." And, also as Isaiah says, chapter 53:6: "Every one turned to his own way." But God's way, which the Scriptures teach, and which is Christ himself, the Son of God, no one goes. And the evil is the greater, since every one, with a word, might be directed to find it.

As in the time of Elijah, not God, but Baal is worshipped. And, as in the time of John the Baptist, when the world was full of sects, and each one wanted to have the preference over the other, so it is now. And even dead saints, and actually wood and stone, and, as was seen here in Mansfeld, a willow stock which they called Gedut, and the holy wolf, which is said to have been a dead dog, are worshipped, and from them comfort and help are invoked, as has also taken place in other lands. And the strong pillars of the Antichristian Church, the miserable theologians of Lyons, in their articles, endeavor to establish and maintain these things.

When we consider the strange and wonderful sects that existed in the time of John, we find them to have been child's play in contrast with the wretched abominations of the monks, nuns, cardinals, bishops, and crowds of ecclesiastics, no one of whom holds with the other; each sect sets up its own god, its own works, rules and orders by which they desire to be saved. Faith in Jesus Christ is, with them, entirely too mean, and men must have a greater and far superior method of salvation, than that which the dear Son of God has taught us.

The state of the Church, where the Pope reigns in person, was still more sad, as facts prove, before God raised up for us the dear man, who, in our times, was a true Elijah and John the Forerunner. For, as Elijah in his time attacked idolatry and overthrew it, so also Dr. Martin Luther attacked the powerful idol, papal indulgences, and struck it to the ground. And as Elijah destroyed the priests of Baal, so this man of God, with the sword of the Divine Word, beat down the mass-saying priests and their darling idol.

But further, like John the holy Baptist, he taught and

preached genuine Christian repentance, how, and by what means men can come to the true knowledge of sin, how forgiveness of sins may be obtained, what are the genuine fruits of repentance, how we should worship God and serve Him, what states God ordained in His Church, what duties each in his particular office must perform. In short, by him God opened the Holy Scriptures, which were before a shut and sealed book, so that never since the time of the Apostles have they been read with such understanding as now.

We have now the knowledge of the real difference between the law and the Gospel, what each is, what they work, how we may use them for our salvation, what are good works, how they please God, why we should exercise ourselves in them, what follows them according to God's promise. This knowledge was very precious to the venerable fathers, such as Jerome, Cyprian, Tertullian and others. But, during the several hundred years of popery, it had so entirely declined that men could have no certain consolation for the conscience in times of temptation or in the hour of death. The monks directed dying persons to the Virgin Mary for consolation. They sang to the people: "*Maria mater graciæ, mater misericordiæ, tu nos ab hoste protege, in hora mortis suscipe.*" That is, "O! Mary, who art the mother of grace and mercy, deliver us from our enemies, and receive us in the hour of death." Or they referred them to other saints, to their orders, and to their good

works. This the true saints never desired. As the
troubled conscience had no certain ground of consolation, they finally died in despair on account of their sins.

Now, however, we have a true and certain ground of
hope, for we live and die in Jesus Christ, the Son of
God, our Lord and Saviour. We sing with Simeon:
"*Nunc dimittis servum tuum Domine in pace.*" [In peace
and joy I go hence, at the will of God.] With holy
Stephen we say: "Lord Jesus, receive my spirit." And
we know, with St. Paul, that "whether living or dying,
we are the Lord's."

What has taught us the blessed art of peaceful dying,
and made known to us the ground of safety, against
which all the gates of hell cannot prevail, out of crosses
and sufferings to draw consolation and joy, and that
changes death into a gentle, peaceful, wholesome sleep?
Under the Gospel, blessed be God, multitudes of people, old and young, and especially this man of God, as
we shall hear, have experienced no fear of death; many
with songs on their lips, many with earnest desire, calling on the name of the Lord, have joyfully yielded
themselves to death.

Of course, this blessed art of peaceful dying we have
not learned from the Pope, who would rather that we
should trust in his indulgences, and die in his favor, and
thus be forever lost. He cares most of all that he may
lead an easy Epicurean life in earthly riches and dignity.
But even this we do not learn from the bishops, for they

neither preach nor visit the sick. The monks would rather bury us in their orders, and in their friar's cowl, than that we should die in Christ. By their aid we would never find the true way to eternal life.

Thanks be to God, the Father of our Lord Jesus Christ, that, out of His infinite grace and mercy, He has by His Holy Spirit enlightened and awakened this, His faithful servant, who, with all diligence and faithfulness, preached, by means of the Gospel, the Son of God, who bruised the head of the old Serpent, that is, delivered us from the power of the Devil, and said to death: "O! death, where is thy sting? O! grave, where is thy victory? The sting of death is sin, and the power of sin is the law, but thanks be to God, which giveth us the victory, through our Lord Jesus Christ." This it is which this man taught, and those who believed derived courage therefrom against sin, death, hell and the Devil.

Well, the man who, in our times, acted in the spirit and power of Elijah, and who was also a true John the Forerunner, before the coming of the last day, is now gone from us, and we will see him no more until the end of the world. Therefore, we too, like Elijah the prophet, may cry: "My father, my father, the chariot of Israel, and the horsemen thereof." With the disciples of John we may also "take up the body and bury it, and come and tell Jesus." But we should not omit to pray, with Elisha, that a double portion of his spirit may be upon us, and to take up the mantle of our Elijah, as it fell from him when he ascended. This mantle is composed of his books which he wrote by the aid of the Holy Spirit, and has left behind him, and out of them we can draw the inspiration of his spirit. If he is dead according to the body, he still lives in the spirit, and in his books. By his writings, too, he is doing God's will, even when dead. He is the death of the Pope, as during his life he was his plague. May we now hold fast to the doctrines of his books, and love and honor them, since they lead us to the Holy Scriptures, and thank God for them.

Let this suffice for the first part of my sermon, in which we have considered what a great man Dr. Martin Luther was, and why we should respect and honor him, namely: Because he was, for our time, an Elijah and John the Forerunner, not a common preacher like myself, and those like me, but a great and renowned man, by whom God has again purified His Church, and graciously endowed it with the pure doctrine, and the true way to worship God.

Second. We will now describe the manner of his death. He is not yet buried, and has been only one day dead. There are already persons, as I am informed, who, driven by the evil spirit, have published the report that we found him dead in his bed. I have no doubt that he who was a liar from the beginning will invent many other and more atrocious calumnies. For he has now no more to do with Dr. Luther, whom God has snatched away from his teeth, and he is beyond his reach. But he is now busy with his doctrine, which he would fain injure, and if possible, destroy. In order to meet him, and to guard believers against his lies, I, as one who was present at the moment of his death, and for three weeks before was with him day and night, will relate the truth concerning his death, here in God's house, and before God himself.

Dr. Martin, my dear friends, did not begin the night past to die, but he was dying for more than a year past. That is, he thought of death, preached about death, conversed about death, wrote about death. Just the day before his departure I read to him, at his request, many consoling passages from his Psalter, which he had marked and written in it, in order to comfort himself with them. He had often prayed to God, and plead that He would, the sooner the better, take him out of this evil world, as he was disgusted and weary of this life. He had often prayed, also, that if it pleased God he might not suffer long on his sick bed. He felt as an old, overworked, feeble man; therefore, he often said, "I will not live much longer," and particularly, just before his death, he said, "If the Pope or my adversaries could get me in their power and inflict upon me much suffering, I am so weak that I would soon die in their hands."

As he was, in all respects, well prepared for death, God graciously heard his sighs and prayers. After he had partaken of his supper, here at Eisleben, and went from the large room into his small room, on the 17th of

February, about 8 o'clock in the evening, and as his cus-
tom was, laid himself down in the window and offered
his prayers, he began in a short time to complain of
great pain in the breast. He was rubbed with warm
cloths, and grated unicorn root administered internally,
with wine. He became better and laid down on the sofa
and went to sleep. He slept until the clock struck ten.
He then awoke and asked Dr. Jonas and myself, who
watched with him, why we did not lie down? We answered
that it was proper that we should wait upon him.

He then arose and did not complain particularly any
more, and went into his chamber to his bed. As he
crossed the threshold of the room, he said: "*In manus
tuas commendo tibi spiritum meum, redemisti me Domine
Deus veritatis.*" That is, "Into Thy hands I commend my
spirit, Thou hast redeemed me, O Lord God of Truth."
He then laid down in his bed, gave us good night and said:
"Dr. Jonas and Mr. Michel, pray to our Lord God that
it may go well with His cause and the Holy Gospel, for
those who are assembled in the Council of Trent do not
mean it well therewith."

He again fell asleep and rested naturally; no change
could be noticed until the clock struck one, past mid-
night. He then awoke and called his family servant and
directed that the small room should be made warm for
him. As it had been kept warm, he raised himself up,
got out of bed, and said: "O, Dr. Jonas, I am in great
pain, I fear I will remain at Eisleben." With this he re-

entered the small room. As he recrossed the threshold he repeated the words he uttered before: "*In manus tuas commendo tibi spiritum meum, redemisti me, Domine Deus veritatis.*" After he walked back and forth once or twice, in this small room, he lay down again on the sofa. His sickness increased and became more and more severe. We immediately rubbed him with warm cloths, and sent for the host of the house, the two city physicians, and at the same time a message was dispatched to his Highness, Count Albrecht, Count and Lord of Mansfeld. Dr. Jonas, and I Michael Celius, and John Aurifaber, together with his family servant, were with him from the beginning. Very soon came the host and his wife, then one of the physicians, and immediately thereafter the other physician, and following them came Count Albrecht and his wife, the Countess.

As we were rubbing him with warm cloths, I asked him if he felt any relief. He answered, "Yes, the warmth does me good; warm also pillows and lay them on me, the pressure on my breast is very great; however, the pain has not yet reached my heart." As I felt with my hand that his linen was quite wet, I said to him: "Reverend father, you are now perspiring; God will be favorable to us, and you will be better." "Yes," he answered, "it is the cold sweat of death; I will die; I will go hence." As, at his request, a sip of wine was given him, and one of the physicians administered a spoonful of medicine, he began to speak and to say:

"I thank Thee, O God, the Father of our Lord Jesus Christ, that Thou hast revealed Thy Son to me, on whom I have believed, whom I have loved, whom I have preached, confessed and worshipped, whom the Pope and all the ungodly abuse and slander. O, my Lord Jesus Christ, I commend my poor soul to Thee."

"O heavenly Father, I know, that although I shall be taken away from this life, I will live forever with Thee."

"*Sic Deus dilexit mundum, ut unigenitus filium suum daret, ut omnis qui credit in eum non pereat, sed habeat vitam æternam.*"

That is: "God so loved the world that he gave his only begotten son, that whosoever believeth in him should not perish, but have everlasting life."

He spake further: "*Deus, noster Deus salvos faciendi, tu es Deus qui educis ex morte.*"

That is: "God, our God, saveth us; Thou art God, who delivereth us from death."

As he now felt that the end was not far off, he spoke three times the words: "*Pater, in manus tuas commendo tibi spiritum meum.*" That is: "Father, into Thy hands I commend my spirit." Thereupon, he suddenly became silent. We shook him and Dr. Jonas and I called loudly to him: "Reverend father, do you die in the faith of your Lord Jesus Christ, and in the doctrine which you preached in His name?" He answered, "Yes." He then turned upon his right side and fell into a few minutes sleep. As we did not trust this sleep, we wetted his face with *aqua vitæ* and vinegar of roses, and rubbed his wrists at the pulse. When the clock stood at a quarter before 3 o clock in the morning, as we were standing looking at him, he heaved a deep breath, and then yielded up his spirit, softly, peacefully, and in much patience, into the hands of his God.

This statement God knows to be true, as we have conscientiously related it. And we are ready to testify in the great day of the Lord, that thus and not otherwise occurred his departure from us. The same is embodied in a history of the occasion, and will appear more fully in print.

I have thus related these facts at length for several reasons. First, to silence the malicious falsehoods of the Devil and his agents. If any other account than that which you have now heard should come to your ears, give·it neither faith nor attention. I and the others who were present are living witnesses of the facts. If any will believe us, well and good; but if any will not believe us, he must be permitted to go his way, to lie and deceive on his own venture. He will finally find his Judge. I know, praised be God, that I have borne true witness.in what I have here said.

Second. I have related this history that we also may learn to prepare for the last hour, and be as ready for it as was this, our faithful teacher and shepherd. For notwithstanding we all know that we must die, yet very few prepare themselves so well for it, that they can in faith, and with willingness, yield themselves to it. We have, however, seen in this man, who was a learned Doctor of the Holy Scriptures, endowed with many gifts, which he devoted to the benefit of others, that he employed himself for a long time with thoughts of death, summed together many passages of the Holy Scriptures for his own consolation, meditated upon it, spoke often with others about it, and yet all the while he faithfully discharged the arduous duties of his office. Then, when he came to the hour in which he as yet knew not how he should die, he was as one who falls asleep, not knowing when or how, but happily and sweetly he sunk to rest. This blessed art of dying we too may learn from this history.

As we have now heard, briefly and simply, who Dr. Martin Luther was, how he died, and what we should learn therefrom, that it may become serviceable, and be made profitable to our salvation and Christian life, we will now, in the third place, consider: Why he was just now, at this critical time, called from us, when his presence in the Christian Church seems so very indispensable, since the Pope and his Council of Trent, and all the gates of Hell are arrayed against the Word and truth of God, which He has revealed by this, His servant and Apostle, in order to suppress and destroy it.

Many reasons might here be assigned to you for his death. Some say that an old man should not have undertaken such an overland journey in such a cold season.

He ought to have been spared the necessity of mediating in the affairs of the Counts. Had he remained at Wittenberg, and kept himself unexposed there, he might be alive now. It is true, that in reason these thoughts and this language must remain unanswered. But if we give way to such ideas, they will lead us into the wild waves of the sea, and like the same, driven about by the wind, there will be no rest for the mind. We must, therefore, abandon these thoughts, for they conduct to no tranquillity or peace, in this case, or in any other cases.

It is best for us, in this case, to confess the faith of our childhood and say: "I believe in God the Father, Almighty Maker of heaven and earth," which is to be understood, not only that God created the heaven and the earth, but that He at the same time preserves and governs them, and that without His will not a hair of our heads can fall to the ground, as Christ has taught, Luke 21:15. So David also, in the 39th Psalm, v. 4., "Lord make me to know mine end, and the measure of my days what it is; that I may know how frail I am." Job also says the same, Chapter 14:5: "Seeing his days are determined; the number of his months are with Thee, Thou hast appointed his bounds that he cannot pass." By these words the Holy Ghost leads us away from the thoughts which our worldly reason had suggested, and helps us out of the wild waves of the sea into a sure haven of rest and peace. We must therefore say: "It is the will of God. He has so ordered it, that in this town of

Eisleben, where he was born and baptized, he should close his life."

But why did God call him at this present time? is another question. The Holy Scriptures assign more than one reason why each one dies at his appointed time. Sometimes God takes to himself the little children soon after their baptism, besides young persons, also. The reason is indicated in the Book of Wisdom: God calls them that wickedness may not pervert their understanding, nor false doctrine deceive their souls. Evil examples mislead and corrupt the good in them, and enticing lusts of the flesh lead guileless hearts astray. God loves them; therefore, he hastens with them out of this evil life.

This gives blessed comfort to parents, who mourn the early death of their children. It is beyond measure painful to reason and nature, when children and young persons are seen to fall into death, around whom so many hopes had clustered. The father had intended to rear his son to an honorable manhood; the mother to bring up her daughter to be a virtuous woman; but dear Lord, we everywhere see how the world tempts to evil with bad examples. Satan is tireless in corrupting principles and life. We have a poor, frail human nature, that is so sadly corrupted by original sin, that, notwithstanding indeed Baptism has covered it, yet, like a fire covered with ashes, so sin still remains in our nature. As when in the morning the housemaid stirs the ashes the fire is kindled afresh, so when a person arrives at years of reason the concealed fires of orignal sin are kindled into a blaze by the Devil, the World, and our own evil lusts blowing upon them. God often comes beforehand, and through death snatches the dear children, in their innocence, from the evil to come. Therein mourning parents may greatly comfort themselves.

So, too, God often removes tyrants. Thus Pharaoh was drowned in the Red Sea; Sennacherib was murdered in the house of his idol god by his own sons; Nero stabbed himself; Julian was shot in the Persian war. Thereby God preserves His Church, that His Word and Kingdom may not be utterly exterminated, as His enemies had designed. These examples are also written for our encouragement, since we, too, see in our times men in high places who persecute the Gospel and its adherents. We may know that God still lives, will protect His Church and overthrow the Pharaoh's and other tyrants that oppressed it. His hand is not short nor His power weak. He knows well how to protect His own and to overthrow tyrants.

But when the Prophets die and are called away by the Lord, His purpose usually is that a chastisement shall follow. He often promises in the Scriptures to protect His people in life, but to avenge them after their death. So when Samuel the Prophet died, the Philistines fell upon the country, captured many cities in which the Israelites dwelt, killed Saul and his three sons, and slaughtered a large number of the people. So, too, after the death of the other Prophets, the Babylonish captivity followed. And after all the Apostles were called away, except John, who alone remained alive, then took place the destruction of Jerusalem, together with the entire Jewish nation, which continues to this day, and until the last day the Jews will not be restored to their land, to their national polity, nor to their divine service.

The cause of all these calamities was their refusal to hear the warning voice of the Prophets, of Christ, and of His Apostles. On the contrary, they reviled and persecuted them, and the more so because His rod was long withheld, and the deserved reward of their iniquities did not speedily follow. We read in 2 Chron. 36:15, 16: "The Lord God of their fathers, sent to them by His messengers, rising up betimes and sending, because He had compassion on His people, and on His dwelling place; but they mocked the messengers of God, and despised His words, and misused His Prophets, until the wrath of the Lord arose against His people, until there was no remedy."

It is greatly to be feared that God has called home this His servant on account of our sins. For he faithfully preached true repentance and forgiveness of sins, according to the command of Christ and the teachings of the Holy Scriptures. He exposed the abuses in the Church. He warned against idolatry. He taught how God should be worshipped and what Christian liberty is.

For all this the World should have knelt down and thanked God. But the Papists, on the contrary, hated him most bitterly, sought to destroy him, reviled his doctrines as heresy, and treated him as if the earth did not bear on its surface so vile a man. This is the way they thanked God for His benefits.

We, on the other hand, who adhere to his doctrine, and are taunted as being Evangelical, entertain for him more fitting sentiments. We know the way of the Lord, for He has revealed it to us by His Word; but we walk according to our own pleasure. In the youth we see neither sense of shame nor propriety of conduct, nor obedience to superiors. In the old, there appear only avarice, love of usury and want of integrity. No one lives any more honestly and uprightly, neither do any take pleasure in their regular calling. Everywhere is fulfilled the lament of the Prophet Hosea, in which he describes the way the people lived in his time, before the Babylonish captivity. He says: chapter 4:1–3, "Hear the Word of the Lord, ye children of Israel: for the Lord hath a controversy with the inhabitants of the land, because there is no truth, nor mercy, nor knowledge of God in the land. By swearing, and lying, and killing, and stealing, and committing adultery, they break out, and blood toucheth blood. Therefore, shall the land mourn, and every one that dwelleth therein shall languish with the beasts of the field, and with the fowls of heaven: yea, the fishes of the sea also shall be taken away."

It is now high time that we should repent and weep, not on account of the death of this blessed man, who is taken away from all this evil, and who rests peacefully in the Lord; but because, by our sins, we have offended God, and are hastening by rapid strides to their punishment. But I am afraid that, in the case of many, the prediction of the Prophet will be verified, and they will not take anything to themselves. For he says, "the righteous perisheth and no man layeth it to heart; and merciful men are taken away, none considering that the righteous is taken away from the evil to come." God's judgments will fall upon the heads of many of the despisers and impenitent, as he is now taken away, and is not permitted to see their misery.

Therefore be admonished, my dear Christian hearers, and whoever has not hitherto laid it to heart, let him now set about it earnestly, hear and give attention to God's Word, repent and be converted, each one turn away from his evil ways, so will the Lord repent of the evil which He had thought to do unto them. But if the ungodly will not have it otherwise, the righteous will be delivered, if not here in time, yet there in eternity. Whilst the ungodly suffer temporal and eternal torments, to us who live a penitent life, the temporal calamities which we endure will even prove a furtherance unto eternal blessedness. In the midst of such calamities the Son of God will preserve His Church, believers will still remain in it, and they will be delivered. But our sinful lives, which God purposed to punish, is the reason of this death.

Let us now, in the fourth and last place, hear what is now the state and condition of this man. Concerning the body, as we yet see it on the bier before us, he sleeps well. He sleeps now a softer sleep than he slept at anytime in his life before. He will sleep this sleep until he shall awake at the last day. He is now free from all care, labor, fatigue and danger. He now fears not Pope, nor Cardinal, the World, nor the Devil. Oh, how did the Pope, and those belonging to him, grieve and put to the rack his pious, faithful, God-fearing heart, with their ungodly ways, in that he was compelled to see the Church and all true worship of God oppressed, and everything filled with vain idolatry and hellish sodomy. In addition to this he was outlawed and banned; his image was burned at Rome, and they would much rather have burned his body. But God mercifully snatched him out of their bloody hands, and laid him in his peaceful rest. They will now, perhaps, leave him undevoured, for he is now "entered into peace, he shall rest in his bed."

It is very consoling to all believers, that the Holy Ghost calls the death of the righteous, that is, believers, "entering into peace," and "resting in their beds." God utters the same truth by the same Prophet, Isaiah 26:20: "Come, my people, enter thou into thy chambers and shut thy doors about thee; hide thyself as it were for a little moment, until the indignation be overpast." Human reason shudders at death, since it sees in it nothing but horror and gloom. But the Scriptures call it a sleep, the believers' peaceful rest in their beds. They sometimes rest indeed before death, as when God imparts to them such great comfort that they are able to disregard the malice of Satan and the World, but whilst in life they rest in a strange chamber, in a strange inn, where one awakes and suffers still the afflictions and persecutions of the World, so this dear man often experienced, and even here at Eisleben, shortly before his happy death, he had joy; but it was in a strange lodging place. Therefore, too, his sufferings were of a short duration. One evening he lamented with tears, that, although he had lifted his heart with joy to God, and prayed, as was his wont, looking out of the window, and up to heaven, he could still perceive that Satan was waiting with open mouth to hinder all his proceedings; but he knew full well that God would be stronger than Satan. .

Whilst God granted him rest, that is, comfort in his heart, still he was not yet at rest in his bed. His rest was distured by Satan, and he was wakened up. But now he has peace and rest in his bed and his rest will henceforth no more be disturbed. Like all the faithful from Adam to the present time, who have gone to sleep in Jesus, he rests softly and still. In the words of the Psalmist: "The sun shall not smite him by day, nor the moon by night." And although he, and we all, shall be consumed of worms, and having been created of the dust, shall return to dust again; still it takes place without any feeling, without pain, without suffering. As St.

Paul teaches us: "It is sown in corruption, it is raised in incorruption. It is sown in dishonor, it is raised in glory. It is sown in weakness, it is raised in power. It is sown in a natural body, it is raised a spiritual body."

Concerning the state of the body of our dear master and father, after his happy death, it is sufficient to say, that we with our bodies and the bodies of all believers will, at the last day, be seen rising again with bodies like unto that which Christ brought with him, as on the first Easter morning he arose from the tomb. They will be more brilliant than the sun, in the clear light of heaven; more swift and active than the wind, and more powerful than all creatures. None shall be able any more to attack, or grieve, or put to death the body. On the contrary, as all things are put under the feet of the Son, so will also Death, the Devil, and Hell, and all creatures be subject to him, and to us. With these words we may comfort ourselves, at this peaceful corpse, and at our own death.

As to what relates to the spirit or soul, we are not of the opinion, as some fanatical spirits put forth, that the spirits or souls of men are in a state of sleep until the last day. The soul was not in a state of sleep whilst in the body, as in a prison and clogged with chains. Shall the soul now be in a state of sleep, when released from out its prison? God did not create the soul with such a nature and with such properties that it should sleep. On the contrary, it always lives and wakes, and works. Even when the body sleeps the soul is awake, as we experience in dreams, and in many other ways. It is therefore an error, as some assert, that the soul, like the body, will sleep until the last day. On the contrary, this is certain, that the soul is awake and lives. As the soul lived before it came to the body, and made the body living, so it lives after its dissolution from the body, and by the powerful hand of God will make the same body living when at the great day it will again come to the body.

With this the Holy Scriptures accord. Abraham, Luke 16, conversed with the rich man in Hell, who saw Lazarus in his bosom. This a sleeper or a dead person cannot do. In Rev. 6:9, 10, the souls that were slain for the Word of God cried with a loud voice, which shows that they were living and awake. Christ says, "God is not the God of the dead, but of the living." God is the God of Abraham, Isaac and Jacob, therefore they must be living. As to the body they were then already a long time dead; it was therefore their souls that lived. They certainly live with God and our Lord Jesus Christ.

It is written, Eccles. 12:7, "The dust shall return to the dust as it was, and the spirit shall return unto God who gave it." To the malefactor Jesus said, "To-day thou shalt be with me in Paradise." St. Paul says, "We are willing to be absent from the body, and present with the Lord." Again, "Whether we live or die we are the Lord's." In Rev. 6:10, 11, we learn that the souls un-

der the altar who were slain for the Word of God cried
with a loud voice and said: "How long, O Lord, holy
and true, dost thou not judge and avenge our blood on
them that dwell on the earth? And white robes were
given unto every one of them, and it was said unto them,
that they should rest for a little season until their fellow-
servants also, and their brethren, that should be killed
as they were, should be fulfilled."

From these and other passages, it is clear that the
souls of the dead live and are awake. Otherwise they
could not cry with a loud and intelligent voice, nor be
with God, or with our Lord Jesus Christ, who is the
altar. From which it follows, that as this servant of
God died, calling on God and confessing the name of
Christ, his spirit is with God and His Son, and exists,
being among the holy angels and the elect of God. As
during his life he was especially in communion with
Moses, Elijah, the Prophets, the Apostles, and particularly St. Paul, whose books had been obscured and
lay in darkness until he, in the spirit of Elijah, with
preaching and writing, again brought them into the light,
and to the right use by the Church, so he is now with them
and with the Lamb, who is in the midst of them, whom
they follow wheresoever he goeth, and whom in life they
knew and confessed. This, too, will we see and experience, when our merciful God, the Father of our Lord
Jesus Christ, shall also call us happily to follow him there.

Having now heard who Dr. Martin Luther was, a true Elijah and John the Baptist for our times, how like a Christian he fell asleep in the Lord, and why God at this time called him out of the World, and also what his present state and condition is, we will commend him to the Lord, and pray that God will send to his Church in his stead another Prophet, and after this Elijah give us an Elisha, who may have a double portion of his spirit, and requite Romish Babylon two fold more than before. And at the same time we pray that the Holy Ghost may enlighten us by means of his books, lead us into the true knowledge of the Holy Scriptures, and into the true faith and holy living, so that we may peacefully close the last hour of earth. Amen.

www.ingramcontent.com/pod-product-compliance
Lightning Source LLC
Chambersburg PA
CBHW031755090426
42739CB00008B/1021